WILDFLOWERS
and the stories
behind their names

And he is happier who has power
To gather wisdom from a flower.
—William Wordsworth

by PHYLLIS S. BUSCH
paintings by ANNE OPHELIA DOWDEN

WILDFLOWERS

and the stories behind their names

Charles Scribner's Sons   *New York*

To my very dear friend and botany professor
Harold H. Clum

All plants pictured in this book—except enlarged details—are
exactly 4/5 actual size.

SEPARATIONS AND PRINTING BY PEARL PRESSMAN LIBERTY
BINDING BY A. HOROWITZ & SON

Printed in the United States of America

Acknowledgments

I am very grateful for all the help that I received from Anne B. Smith and from Frank Anderson of the New York Botanical Garden. I am especially indebted to Connie Campbell, whose knowledge and enthusiasm served to guide me to the wonderful resources of the Arents Collections at the New York Public Library.

I would be remiss if I did not acknowledge that the "birth" of the idea for this book was stimulated by the article "The Names of Nature," by Charles Scribner, Jr., which appeared in *National Wildlife* 10, no. 3 (April-May 1972).

Phyllis S. Busch

The artist wishes to thank the following for assistance in collecting living specimens of plants: Professors Frederick S. Page and James P. Poole, Dartmouth College; Mr. Frederick McGourty, Brooklyn Botanic Garden; Professor Eville Gorham, University of Minnesota; Mr. John Moore, Denver, Colorado; Mr. and Mrs. Herman Freudenberg, Boulder, Colorado; Mr. Robert Moeller, Sharon, Connecticut; and especially her husband Raymond B. Dowden.

Anne Ophelia Dowden

Contents

Introduction – The Naming of Plants

Plants have always played a vital part in our lives. Think of the different kinds of plant foods that you eat every day—salad greens, peanut butter, rice, fruit, and many more. Appropriately, the word *botany*, meaning plants, comes from the Greek word *boskein*, "to feed."

Since ancient times, plants and their juices have also been used to prevent or cure sickness. Plants are a source of products such as wood, dyes, rubber, perfume, tar, fibers, and cosmetics. But perhaps their most delightful contribution is the pleasure and inspiration that plants and the knowledge of plants have brought to artists, poets, storytellers, or anyone who has ever stopped to admire the wonder of a wildflower.

Who was it who first named these plants that are so important to our lives? What did they call them, and why? Certainly in this country it was the native Indians who gave names to the plants they used and enjoyed, as well as the early settlers from Europe. Indeed, many of our plants, along with their

1

common names, were brought to America by the first settlers. Most likely, those people who were intimately involved with plants in their work and surroundings were the original plant namers—farmers, hunters, woodsmen, medicine men. When you consider the pictorial imagery of some of these names—Jack-in-the-pulpit, Buttercup—you can see that these people also had a touch of the poet in them.

Most common names usually describe something about the plant: its color or scent, where it is found, what familiar object it resembles, or what it is used or might be used for. Sometimes the name is the result of a story, a myth, or a legend. The plant name may include several of these references. For example, the name Buttercup suggests that the flower has a shape like a cup and is the color of butter. Bedstraw is the common name of a plant that was once used for stuffing mattresses and pillows.

Thousands of such descriptive names were given to plants, and they continue to be used to this day. The only difficulty is that the same plant might have a number of different common names, depending on where it is found and what the local people originally called it. Queen Anne's Lace is the common plant name in one location. Elsewhere this plant is known as Bird's Nest, and in another place, Wild Carrot.

In order to avoid confusion, a plant-naming system was developed by a Swedish botanist, Carolus

Linnaeus. His system was published in 1758. Plants were grouped according to their structural likenesses. Then each plant was assigned two names. This scientific system of naming plants, still in use today, is known as the binomial (two-name) system. The two names are almost always in Latin. The first name is always capitalized, and indicates the group or genus to which the plant belongs. The second name is the descriptive word, usually an adjective. Together, the two names identify a given plant as a species. No two species have the same two words in their name. Thus, while scientists in different parts of the world may not know what plant is meant by Queen Anne's Lace, Bird's Nest, or Wild Carrot, they will readily recognize it by its scientific name, *Daucus carota*.

Though I have included the scientific names for each of the fifty plants in this collection, the first concern of this book is the common plant name and the story behind it. Sometimes, of course, this involves the scientific name as well. Today, especially among city dwellers, the names of plants are too often taken for granted and their meanings forgotten. There is poetry, humor, history, and even a mystery or two in these names.

What's in a name? That which we call a Rose
By any other name would smell as sweet.

—William Shakespeare, *Romeo and Juliet*

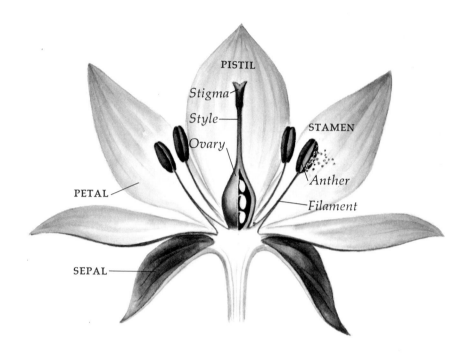

Parts of a Flower

The function of flowers is to produce seeds from which new plants may grow. Although there is great variety among flowers they all have basic structural likenesses.

The *Stamen* is the male sex organ. It consists of a *Filament*, which supports an *Anther*. Inside the anther are found grains of *Pollen*, which contain the male sex cell or sperm cell.

4

The *Pistil* is the female sex organ. Its top bears a sticky or feathery *Stigma*, which is connected by a passageway, the *Style*, to the *Ovary*. The ovary has one or more *Ovules*. Inside each ovule is a female sex cell, or egg.

Stamens and Pistils are surrounded by *Petals* whose bright colors, odors, and shapes are attractive to certain birds, insects, and small mammals. As these animals forage among the flowers for nectar or pollen, they may brush off pollen from the anthers of one flower and carry it to the stigma of another flower of the same kind. The pollen then grows down to and into the ovule. There the male and female sex cells unite and the ovule develops into a seed. The ovary around it forms a fruit.

The *Sepals* form an envelope around the base of the flower. When the flower is in bud, the sepals cover and protect it from drought, heavy rain, and insects. Sepals are usually green; however, in some flowers the sepals are the same color as the petals and might be mistaken for petals.

Wild Geranium or Cranesbill

From the middle of spring and well into summer along roadsides and in open woodland you'll find the beautiful Wild Geranium *(Geranium maculatum)*. The parts of this flower are easy to observe. There are five green sepals, five pink or purplish petals, ten stamens, and five parts to the pistil in the center.

Find a plant that has some blossoms on it as well as some fruit or seed pods. The seed pod that forms after flowering is completed looks like the beak of a bird. It was thought to resemble that of a crane, and this is how the scientific and common names originated. *Geranium* comes from the Greek word *geranos*, which means crane's bill.

FLOWER MASS
INSIDE HOOD

Skunk Cabbage

If you call out, "I smell skunk!" as you are walking
through a marshy woodland or a wet meadow, you
may be passing by a plant called Skunk Cabbage
(*Symplocarpus foetidus*). A rank smell, which resembles the scent produced by a frightened skunk,
escapes from any part of the Skunk Cabbage that has
been bruised. The leaves of Skunk Cabbage may
measure up to three feet long and one foot wide and
look like cabbage leaves.

The flowers of the Skunk Cabbage are among
the first to bloom in the spring. They are difficult to

see because they are hidden deep down under a horn-shaped hood. This attractive six-inch hood is purplish brown, or greenish yellow and purple, and often appears above ice and snow as early as February, when nothing else is in bloom.

Daisy and Black-eyed Susan

The word *daisy* comes from two old Anglo-Saxon words, *daeges* and *eage*, which mean day's eye. When the flower of the Daisy (*Chrysanthemum leucanthemum*) first opens, the white circle of petal-like rays unfolds to uncover the yellow center, which is like the sun, the "eye" of the day. Farmers, irritated by the abundance of these plants, call them White-weed. Girls and boys who like to pull off the white rays, in order to find out whether or not their sweethearts love them, have given the plant another common name: Love-me, Love-me-not.

The Black-eyed Susan (*Rudbeckia hirta*) has bright yellow rays around a dark center or eye. The eye, or central disk, is not black at all. If you look closely, you will see brown and dark purple, but never black. In some places people call this flower Brown-eyed Susan or Brown Betty. Another common name is simply Yellow Daisy.

Teasel or Gypsy Comb

Teasel (*Dipsacus sylvestris*) is a very attractive plant —not only when the many purple flowers decorate the egg-shaped flower head, but also later, when the flowers have gone and the bristly two-inch heads are left bare.

These flower heads are dried and used to raise or tease the surface, or nap, of woolen cloth. This process is something like using a comb to tease hair to make it light and fluffy. Perhaps gypsies have used Teasel as a hair comb, since Gypsy Comb is also one of its common names. In industry, dried Teasel heads are attached to a large broad wheel. The woolen cloth is held against the heads as the wheel is turned, thus raising the nap of the cloth.

Always handle Teasel with gloves. There are prickles all over the plant. For this reason cattle may feed around the plant but never on it.

12

Day Lily

Day Lilies grow in large clumps along roadsides and in fields. They add bright touches of orange *(Hemerocallis fulva)* or yellow *(Hemerocallis flava)* wherever you find them. The yellow species is sometimes called the Lemon Lily. It has a lemon scent.

There may be as many as ten buds on one tall stalk, but only one or two open at a time and each lives but one day. The scientific name *Hemerocallis* comes from two Greek words, *hemero* and *kallos*, which together mean "day beauty."

The roots, buds, and flowers are excellent foods, either fresh or dried, and are commonly used in the plant's native home in China, Japan, and Siberia.

FRUIT

FLOWER

Tumbleweed or Russian Thistle or Russian Cactus

Tumbleweeds are plants of the open prairie. In the fall they break off at their roots and roll and tumble in the wind, scattering their hundreds of thousands of seeds. Several kinds of plants that spread their seeds in this way are called Tumbleweeds, but the best known is probably the Russian Thistle (*Salsola kali*). The tumbleweed seed came to this country from Russia, accidentally mixed in with other seeds. It has spread across the land, in waste places and, unfortunately, in cultivated fields as well. It has inconspicuous greenish flowers. The fruits are prettier, each surrounded by a pink ruffle. The leaves are stiff and prickly, which explains the common names Russian Thistle and Russian Cactus.

17

Johnny-jump-up or Wild Pansy or Heartsease

These bright-looking little flowers spring up almost anywhere—gardens, lawns, old battlefields. For this reason they are called Johnny-jump-ups (*Viola tricolor*). They are the wild ancestors of the large cultivated Pansy and are frequently called Wild Pansies. The pattern of rich purple, blue, and yellow forms what looks like a thoughtful, or pensive, little face. The name Pansy comes from the French word *pensée*, meaning thought.

The largest of the five petals has a nectar tube on the end near the stem. If you carefully peel off this petal you can find Johnny seated with his two feet in a "tub." The "feet" are two of the five stamens, and it looks as if Johnny is taking a foot bath. According to some other stories, it is a fairy bathing her tired feet.

Heartsease is a common name that probably originated in England.

> *Heartsease! One could look for half a day*
> *Upon this flower, and shape in fancy out*
> *Full twenty different tales of love and*
> > *sorrow,*
> *That gave the gentle name.*
>
> —Mary Howitt

Witch Hazel

Witch Hazel (*Hamamelis virginiana*) is a tall shrub that puts on a fine show in late autumn. The blossoms at the end of the twigs look like golden threads and give off a very pleasant perfume. These flowers form fruits that take a year to develop. When ripe, the pods burst open and the seeds are ejected for some distance, rattling among the dead leaves. Long ago people who did not know the reason for this scary sound thought that it had something to do with witches. More closely connected with witchcraft was the practice of using a branch of Witch Hazel to find

water. A person called a water witch would walk over a selected area, holding in front of him a forked branch of the shrub. Such branches were also called divining rods. He would twirl the stick between his fingers and recite some strange words. Whenever the forked part of the branch dipped downward, the spot was thought to be a rich source of underground water. The dried leaves and bark of this plant are used to make a liquid preparation also called witch hazel. It is used as an astringent or as an external treatment for bruises and sore muscles.

Butter-and-eggs or Toadflax
Peppergrass or Bird's Pepper

From spring into fall, roadsides and waste places are brightened by spikes of Butter-and-eggs (*Linaria vulgaris*). The plant was given this name because long ago it reminded someone of yellow butter and orange egg yolk. Look closely at the flowers. Each resembles a small yellow mouth with an orange palate, a bit like the mouth of a toad. The leaves of the plant are similar to those of flax, so it is also called Toadflax.

The tiny white flowers on Peppergrass (*Lepidium virginicum*) are hardly noticeable. The round, flat fruits that develop after blooming are much more conspicuous. The biting taste of these little pods explains the common name. The plant grows as freely in the crack of a city sidewalk as along a country road—so free for the taking that some call it Poor-man's Pepper. Since birds often feed on the seeds, the plant is also known as Bird's Pepper. When it rains, the seeds become very sticky and cling to the feet of birds, who unknowingly sow them wherever they walk.

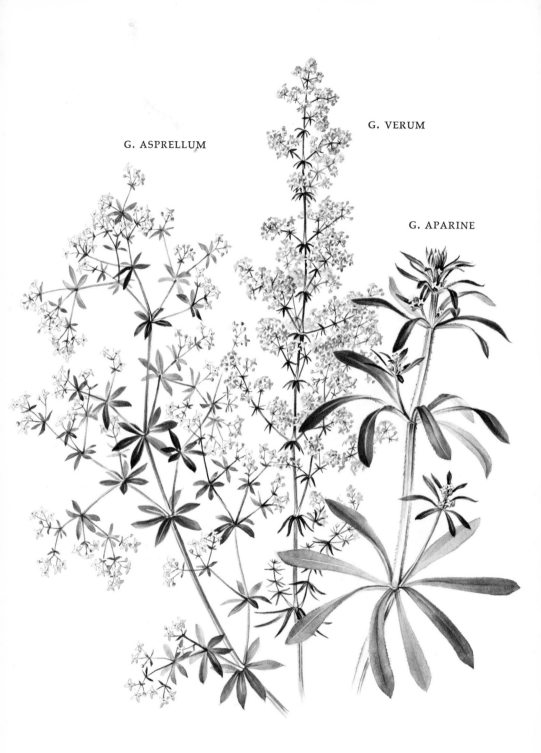

G. ASPRELLUM

G. VERUM

G. APARINE

Bedstraw

People used to gather these plants, dry them, and stuff their mattresses with them. There are many species of bedstraw. It is said that dry Yellow Bedstraw was in the manger where Jesus was born, and that the infant Jesus was laid on these plants by his mother, Mary. For this reason it is sometimes called Our Lady's Bedstraw. Yellow Bedstraw (*Galium verum*) has smooth stems and tiny four-lobed flowers that grow in dense golden clusters. The flowers give off a summery perfume. The entire plant is sweet-smelling, and the fragrance increases as it dries. A very common Bedstraw (*Galium asprellum*) has long, weak stems that lean on other plants and look almost like vines. Its tiny white flowers grow in fluffy clusters. The edges of the leaves are slightly rough and the stems are somewhat prickly. Another white-flowered Bedstraw, commonly called Cleavers (*Galium aparine*), has two tiny white flowers on each stalk. Both the leaves and the stems have prickles and are quite rough. For this reason some people also call it Scratchgrass.

Wild Morning-glory or Hedge Bindweed

The pretty flowers of the Wild Morning-glory (*Convolvulus sepium*) open early and fully on sunny mornings. Long ago people who saw these vines of beautiful flowers named them Morning-glories. Morning-glory blossoms usually close at sunset. But if the moon is full and bright, they may remain open after dark.

26

Morning-glory vines may grow ten or more feet long. They climb over and around, binding any plants they encounter, such as weeds, shrubs, and hedges. This suggested the name Hedge Bindweed. Morning-glory stems are very vigorous and twine so rapidly that you can almost see them grow. A stem might make a complete circle in about two hours.

The large, two-inch flower is either all white or all pink with white stripes, resembling a lady's nightcap, and so the plant is also called Lady's Nightcap.

Heal-all or Self-heal or Carpenter's Weed

People used to believe that for every illness there was a plant that could cure it. Also, the structure of a plant was a guide in determining which ailment it could remedy. For example, if the leaf of a plant resembled the liver, this was considered to be a sign that the plant cured liver diseases. Or, if the root of the plant was shaped like a foot, that plant was used for foot problems.

Heal-all (*Prunella vulgaris*) is a low-growing plant bearing spikes of bluish-purple flowers. Each flower resembles an open mouth leading into a throat, and it was thought the plant was especially good for healing sore throats. However, it was also thought to be helpful in all kinds of sickness, so eventually it became known as Heal-all. In fact, some people thought that they would never need to see a doctor if they had this plant growing nearby. They called the plant Self-heal. It was often used by laborers when they injured themselves at work, so it also became known as Carpenter's Weed.

Compass Plant

One of the tallest flowering plants of the prairies—from Ohio to Alabama and westward to South Dakota and Texas—is the Compass Plant (*Silphium laciniatum*). It has been known to grow as tall as nine feet. The enormous lower leaves stand upright. The edges of these leaves always face north and south, thus acting like a compass. Many a pioneer or traveler used the Compass Plant to find his way across the prairies. The large yellow flower of this tall plant was almost like a signpost, easily spotted in the distance.

> *Look at this vigorous plant that lifts its head*
> *from the meadow,*
> *See how its leaves are turned to the north,*
> *as true as the magnet;*
> *This is the compass flower . . .*
> —Henry Wadsworth Longfellow, *Evangeline*

St. Johnswort

St. Johnswort (*Hypericum perforatum*) is named in honor of Saint John the Baptist. The yellow flowers open on or about the same time as the saint's festival day, June 24. The sun is very high in the sky at this time of year, so Saint John and the plant are considered to be chasers of darkness, of gloom, of evil, of the devil.

If a leaf of St. Johnswort is held against the light, many small, clear dots can be seen. According to legend, these are spots where the devil pricked the plant with a needle. The plant resisted, and from then on the devil feared this plant. People regarded St. Johnswort as holy and believed it would protect them from the devil.

If the plant is bruised, the juice stains the fingers red. This was said to be the blood of Saint John.

Wild Columbine or Rock Bells or Lion's Herb

The common Wild Columbine (*Aquilegia canadensis*) is a colorful red and yellow flower. In days gone by people thought the fluttering flower heads looked like a flock of hovering doves. They named the plant Columbine, which comes from the Latin word *columba* meaning dove.

Lion's Herb is another name given to this plant. According to an old myth, lions ate the flower early in the spring in order to grow stronger. It is also called Rock Bells. The flowers have a bell-like shape, and the plant thrives in rocky soil.

Probably the most exquisite Columbine of all is the graceful, long-spurred blue and white flower known as the Colorado Blue Columbine (*Aquilegia coerulea*). It is sometimes found pure white. It is the state flower of Colorado.

Common Plantain or White-man's Foot

Common Plantain (*Plantago major*), like so many of our other wild plants, immigrated here with the early settlers. Either the seeds were accidentally mixed in with other imported seeds, or they stuck to the feet of cattle or other domesticated animals that were brought over.

Each plant consists of a flat circle of dark green leaves with one or more stalks in the center. All along these three to ten inch spikes grow many tiny greenish flowers. Each flower forms several seeds. When they are wet, the seeds become sticky and cling to the feet of cattle and people as they walk over them. In this way the seeds are transplanted and give rise to new and numerous plants. The scientific name *Plantago* means sole of the foot. It is said that long ago the Indians knew that Common Plantain was not native to their land and used it as a clue or sign in detecting the presence of white men.

We read in *The Song of Hiawatha* by Longfellow:

Wheresoe'er they tread, beneath them
Springs a flower unknown among us,
Springs the White-man's Foot in blossom.

SEED CAPSULE

FLOWER

Jack-in-the-pulpit or Indian Turnip

Jack-in-the-pulpit *(Arisaema triphyllum)* is a fascinating plant. "Jack" is hidden under a flap in a pulpit-like vase that is striped in shades of green and sometimes purple. This vase is not the plant's flower. If the pointed tip of the flap is turned up, Jack can be seen. Jack, the preacher, is the name given to the smooth, shiny club. At the base of this club are the flowers, which are very small indeed. In the autumn, the pulpit is gone and the club displays bright red berries where the flowers grew earlier. These berries were cooked and eaten as a delicacy by the Indians. The Indians also ate the root, boiling it first to destroy its unpleasant taste, and then mashing it up into a nourishing food called Indian Turnip.

Goatsbeard or Go-to-bed-at-noon

This tall yellow flower, which sometimes reaches three feet, looks like a pale, overgrown dandelion. In fact, it is related to the dandelion. When the fruits or seeds have formed, the floral head becomes a gigantic blowball. The large, tough seeds resemble a goat's beard, from which came the common name, Goatsbeard (*Tragopogon pratensis*).

The flower's sleepy behavior is responsible for its other name, Go-to-bed-at-noon. The flower head unfolds in the morning when the sun comes up, then closes up at noon.

The goat's beard, which each morn abroad
    does peep,
But shuts its flowers at noon, and goes to sleep.
—Abraham Cowley

Common Milkweed or Silkweed

The first thing that may attract you to a patch of flowering Milkweed (*Asclepias syriaca*) is its heavy sweet scent. Then you notice the attractive clusters of dull purple and brown flowers that produce this fragance. And looking more carefully among the flowers, you notice a great variety of visitors: bees, beetles, flies, wasps, butterflies. They are guided to the Milkweed by its perfume and remain to dine on its large supply of nectar.

If you examine the underside of the plant's leaves, you may find what looks like a miniature pearl. This is the egg of the monarch butterfly. The young that hatch from it feed on the plant and the plant juices which later protect the mature butterflies,

43

by causing them to be distasteful to birds and other predators. As a result, birds avoid the monarch, along with any other butterfly that resembles the monarch —the viceroy, for example.

If the stem of this plant is bruised, drops of a thick milky liquid drip from the broken surface, suggesting the name Milkweed.

Inside the large, pear-shaped seed pods that form in the fall are dark brown seeds with silken parachutes. On a clear, crisp autumn day, watch for the plumes of Milkweed seeds as they go sailing by. The silk from this plant has been used for stuffing pillows as well as for weaving cloth, and hence its other common name is Silkweed.

Jewelweed or Touch-me-not

Jewelweeds are juicy-stemmed, many-branched native plants that grow to between two and six feet tall. They produce many blossoms all summer long. Some are pale yellow (*Impatiens pallida*) and some are orange, spotted with red (*Impatiens capensis*). The inch-long flowers look like tiny jewels. Dangling from their delicately arched stems, the jewel-like flowers resemble earrings, and are sometimes called Lady's Eardrops.

After the flowers have finished blooming, they are replaced by little seed pods. If you touch the end of a ripened pod, it will pop open and the seeds will shoot out at you. This accounts for its other common name, Touch-me-not, as well as its scientific name, *Impatiens*.

Early in the morning or immediately after a rain, the wet leaves have a silvery shine. If you hold one under water, the leaf appears to turn silver. Because of this, the plant is also called Silverleaf.

Red Clover or Honey Suckers

There are many species of clover, but perhaps Red
Clover (*Trifolium pratense*) presents the loveliest
sight and liveliest sound. Rosy flower heads nod as
bumblebees hum among them. A head of clover is a
collection of many little florets, each one resembling
a miniature sweet pea. Pluck a few and suck them

to taste the sweet nectar. It is no wonder that bees are so active among the clover blossoms, or that the plants are often called Honey Suckers. Only bumblebees and butterflies have mouth parts equipped to reach deep down to the nectar supply.

The word *clover* comes from the Anglo-Saxon word for club—*cloefer*—which refers to the three knotted club belonging to Hercules of Greco-Roman mythology. The design for the club suit in a deck of playing cards is taken from the clover leaf. Clover has been an omen of good fortune since ancient times, especially the rare four-leafed clover.

One leaf for fame,
And one for wealth,
One for a faithful lover,
And one to bring you glorious health,
Are in a four-leaf clover.

Indian Pipe or Ghost Flower

In a dark, gloomy part of the forest, look under the trees among the dead leaves where only a few ferns grow. There you may find the low clusters of white waxy Indian Pipes (*Monotropa uniflora*).

Until the seeds are formed, the flower droops on a long slender stem resembling the peace pipe of American Indian lore. When the seeds begin to form, the plant raises its head.

Because there is an eeriness to its white and waxy look, it is also called Ghost Flower. Another common name is Ice Plant because it feels cold to the touch.

Early in the summer Indian Pipe is faintly pink. Occasionally it remains pink, but more commonly it turns white like a wax candle. Finally it turns black. It will also turn black if picked or touched. Indian Pipe has no green leaves, so it cannot make its own food, as most other plants do. It gets its nourishment from the decaying materials in the rich, moist ground where it grows.

Forget-me-not and Buttercup

Once upon a time, according to an old German legend, a beautiful girl walked with her lover along the banks of the Danube. She saw some bright blue flowers on a little island and expressed a wish for them. Her lover plunged into the water, swam to the island, and picked the blossoms. He started to return, but a swift current overpowered him. As he was swept past his sweetheart to his death, he threw the flowers at her feet, calling out, "Forget me not!" And she never did.

> For the lady fair of her knight so true
> Still resembled the hopeless lot,
> And she cherished the flower of brilliant hue,
> And braided her hair with the blossoms blue,
> And then called it "Forget-me-not."
> —Bishop Mant

The scientific name for Forget-me-not is *Myosotis scorpioides.*

It is an old, old custom to hold the cuplike flower of the Buttercup (*Ranunculus acris*) under a friend's chin. If the yellow of the flower is reflected on his skin, he is supposed to like butter. Another interesting but less familiar name for this plant is Crowfoot. Look closely at the shape of the leaf and you will see the resemblance.

51

Flowering Dogwood or Dagwood or Skewerwood

In some places this beautiful flowering tree or bush is called Dagwood, from the Old English word for dagger. Butchers have used its very hard wood for meat skewers, and thus another common name is Skewerwood. The fact that Indians called it Arrow-wood suggests that they found another use for it. According to one story, the word *dogwood* comes from the practice of using the bark of the tree to make a strong medicine for washing sick dogs. Whatever the name, however, one of the most beau-

tiful sights in spring is the flowering of the Dogwood (*Cornus florida*). The large white bannerlike flowers are not true flowers. They are sets of four attractive bracts which surround the small inconspicuous flowers clustered in the center. These bracts start out as dark purplish bud covers. With the coming of spring they break away at the tips and begin to grow. They turn green, then white or pink. You can see the small brown notch on each bract where it originally broke loose. After the bracts fall off, clusters of bright red fruit replace the center flowers.

Pitcher Plant

We all know that some animals, such as cows and deer, feed on plants and that others, such as hawks and lions, eat other animals. But it may be a surprise to learn that some plants also eat animals. The Pitcher Plant (*Sarracenia purpurea*), which sits low in bogs and mossy swamps, is one of these. It dines on insects.

It is the green of a plant, usually its leaves, which manufactures food. In the Pitcher Plant, the leaves have an additional function. Each of these leaves is about six inches long and is shaped like the spout of a pitcher. The leaves are pale green or green with stripes of yellow and red. These leaf containers always have some water in them. A sweet substance on the edge of the pitcher leaf attracts the insects. As they feed they get trapped by the hairs lining the vessel and they drown in the water below. Gradually the insect bodies turn soft and are digested, then absorbed by the leaves of the plant.

Bouncing Bet or Soapwort

The slightest breeze causes the clusters of pink or white blossoms of the Bouncing Bet plant to bob up and down. This must have suggested to someone long ago a jolly active little girl—Bouncing Bet! Bouncing Bet (*Saponaria officinalis*) grows in large numbers along roadsides July through September. The flowers are mildly fragrant by day, but their perfume increases at nightfall, and they are often pollinated by night-flying moths.

All parts of this plant, and especially the leaves, contain a substance that makes a soapy lather when mixed with water. This gave the plant its genus name, *Saponaria*, from the Latin *sapo*, which means soap, as well as its other common name, Soapwort. Women used it for washing their hair and for laundering fine woolens, linens, and silks. It is still used for such purposes in some countries.

Passionflower or Maypop

The beautiful purple and white Passionflower (*Passiflora incarnata*) is a vining plant of the warm South. Parts of the flower head are thought of as symbols of Christ's sufferings on the cross. This suffering is also known as Christ's Passion. The petals and sepals represent Christ's apostles. The fringe inside the petals and sepals is likened to the crown of thorns that Christ wore. The three sections of the pistil represent the nails of the cross on which he died. Some people see many other religious symbols in other parts of the flower, in its colors, and in its starlike appearance upon opening. Because it begins to bloom in May, this plant is also called Maypop.

Dandelion or Blowball
or Lion's Tooth

The yellow, flowering Dandelion (*Taraxacum officinale*) blooms almost everywhere, every month of the year. It opens each day, but only when the sun shines. It closes at night. The word *dandelion* comes from the French *dent de lion*, which means tooth of the lion. The jagged leaf of the dandelion looks like a row of teeth in a lion's jaw. Examine the rays of this composite flower and you will find that each floret has five little teeth at its edge. These are also compared to the teeth of a lion. The root of the plant is long and sturdy. When pulled up and peeled, it is very white—"as clean as a lion's tooth," some claim.

In the fruiting stage the hundreds of little yellow florets form hundreds of little seeds or fruits. Each has its own parachute. Now the dandelion is an airy, delicate globe, or Blowball. People love to blow on it and make predictions. For example, it is thought that the direction in which the seeds fly shows where your lover is. Or, if you want to know if your sweetheart is thinking of you, blow on a Blowball. If any seeds are left, the answer is yes.

LEAF HAIRS
ENLARGED

Common Mullein or Quaker Rouge or Torch Flower

Quaker girls were forbidden to use face make-up. However, they discovered that by rubbing the leaf of the Common Mullein (*Verbascum thapsus*) lightly on their cheeks, they caused a slight irritation that brought a rosy color to their skin. As this use of the plant became popular, some people called the plant Quaker Rouge. Many years ago people often put Mullein leaves in their shoes because they believed that the slight irritation that resulted would improve their blood circulation. These effects are caused by the downy branching hairs that cover both sides of the Mullein leaves. The hairs make the leaves feel so soft that the plant has also been called Velvet Plant and Flannel Flower. The word *mullein* itself comes from the Middle English word *moleyne*, which means soft.

Hundreds of years ago Roman soldiers broke off the stout, six-foot spikes bearing the bright yellow Mullein flowers, dipped the stalks in melted fat, set them aflame, and used them as torches to light their way. They called the plant Torch Flower.

Dayflower and Shepherd's Purse

The Dayflower (*Commelina communis*) has three petals. Two are bright blue and very colorful. The third is white and frequently goes unnoticed. Although the flowers are in bloom for several months in the late summer, each flower lasts only one day, and thus its common name is Dayflower. The scientific name *Commelina* comes from the Commelyn brothers, three Dutchmen who were all botanists. Two were very ambitious and did a great deal of work. The third worked less hard. It is said that the two bright blue petals represent the hard-working brothers, while the less showy white petal is a symbol of the less ambitious one.

The little, inconspicuous Shepherd's Purse (*Capsella bursa-pastoris*) can be found blooming in some sheltered spot most of the year. It has tiny white flowers, each with four petals. Examine it when its seed pods have formed. A long time ago people thought these pods resembled the leather bags that shepherds used for carrying their meals into the fields, and they named the plant Shepherd's Purse. Others felt the triangular pods were shaped like hearts, and another, less familiar name is Mother's Heart.

SEED POD

Asters and Goldenrods

There are more than a hundred kinds of Asters in the United States. Most of them are blue or purple. There is almost an equal number of different Goldenrods. The spectacular New England Aster (*Aster novae-angliae*) and the noticeably tall Goldenrod

(*Solidago canadensis*) decorate fields and roadsides each autumn. The word *aster* is the same as the Greek and Latin word meaning star. The flower head of the Aster looks like a star, and according to one myth, Asters were created out of stardust. Goldenrods are indeed like rods of gold as they hang heavy with flower. Frequently you will see Goldenrods with galls, or swellings, on their stems. These swellings are caused by a developing gall insect. When mature, the insects leave the gall through a tiny hole.

According to an Indian legend, there were two little girls who were very good friends. As they walked through the fields one day, they talked about what they would like to do when they grew up. One, who had lovely golden hair, said that she would like to do something that would make people cheerful. The other, who had beautiful blue eyes, said that what she wanted most was to be with her golden-haired friend. They met an old Indian squaw and told her their wishes. The squaw gave each one a magic corn cake. After eating the cakes, both girls disappeared. However, the next day, two new kinds of flowers appeared where they had walked: Asters and Goldenrods.

Bluets or Quaker Ladies

If you come across a mass of tiny sky-blue flowers about three to six inches high, with bright yellow centers, you have found some Quaker Ladies, commonly known as Bluets (*Houstonia caerulea*). Everything about these little flowers is delicate—their color, size, and shape. The blossoms with their sweet, upturned faces, reflecting the purity and innocence of a summer sky, may account for the name Quaker Ladies, as well as the less familiar name Innocence.

Hawkweeds: Devil's Paintbrush and King Devil

The Devil's Paintbrush (*Hieracium aurantiacum*) makes a startling summer show of orange-red flowers. The King Devil (*Hieracium pratense*) looks like a yellow copy of the same flower.

At one time it was believed that Hawkweeds could improve a person's eyesight. According to one story, hawks, whose food and survival depend upon their sharp vision, knew this and visited these plants to drink their juice. In fact, it is said that they also taught their young how to use the sap for strengthening their eyesight.

Farmers consider Hawkweeds a nuisance because they spread so readily and are so difficult to remove. Therefore, the Orange Hawkweed is often called the Devil's Paintbrush, or simply Devil's Weed. The Yellow Hawkweed, sometimes called Indian Paintbrush, is more often known as King Devil or Yellow Devil.

Cattail

Cattails are found at the marshy edges of lakes and streams. They usually grow in bunches. The scientific name for the plant is *Typha latifolia*. *Typha* comes from the Greek word *typhe*, meaning cat's tail—a vivid description of these brown tails that grow on tall spikes above pointed green leaves.

In the spring, greenish-yellow male or staminate flowers crowd the upper part of the rounded spike. The mature stamens give off enormous amounts of pollen, which can be collected and used as a flour for bread, cakes, and pancakes. Toward the end of summer these flowers have withered, leaving a rather bare and untidy-looking tail.

Below the male flowers grow the female blossoms. These consist mostly of pistils. As the season advances, this part begins to look like a fuzzy dark brown tail, neat and tidy all along its four- to twelve-inch length.

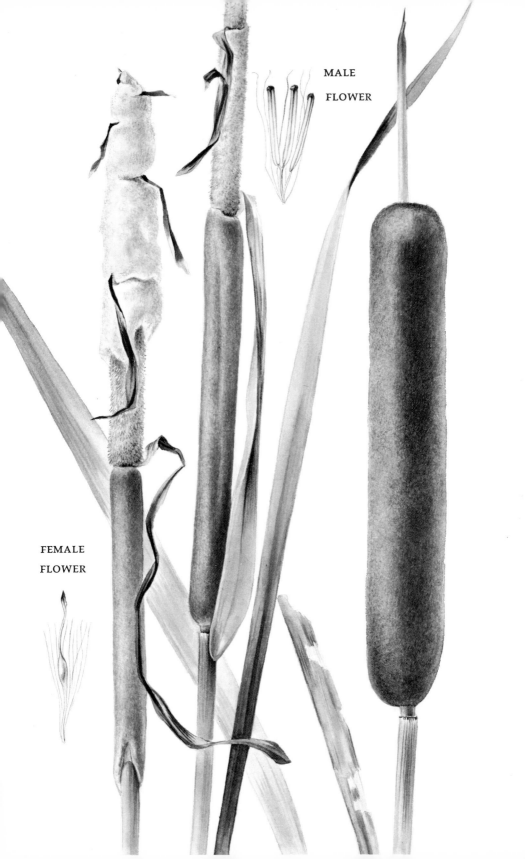

MALE
FLOWER

FEMALE
FLOWER

Chicory or Ragged Sailors

You will find the clear blue flowers of the tall Chicory plant (*Cichorium intybus*) along roadsides, frequently in the company of Queen Anne's Lace. Though usually blue, the flowers are occasionally white and, more rarely, pink. They are at their brightest in the morning. By noon they begin to look worn and ragged, and this, plus their blue color, explains the name Ragged Sailors.

The large root of this plant runs deep underground. When roasted and ground the root can be mixed with coffee or used as a coffee substitute called chicory. The genus name *Cichorium* comes from the Latin *succurrere*, which means to run under.

Groundnut or Rosary Root

The Groundnut (*Apios americana*) is a wild bean vine found in the eastern United States from Michigan to Florida. It gets its name from the long strings of egg-shaped tubers that form along the plant's underground stem. The tubers are edible, cooked or raw, and long ago the Indians cultivated the plant for food. It is said that the abundance of food from this plant saved the lives of the Pilgrims during their first year in America. Early French settlers gave it the name Rosary Root, as the long stem with its

tubers reminded them of a string of rosary beads.

In late summer the vine bears short, thick clusters of pea-shaped blossoms. They are chocolate brown, velvety to touch, and very fragrant. You usually smell the flower before you see it. After the blossoms are gone, bean pods appear, and so the plant is also called Wild Bean. The pods dry and twist open, scattering the bean seeds. The plant reproduces itself from the seeds, as well as the underground tubers.

Velvet-Leaf or Butter-Print or Pie-Marker

It is not the yellow one-inch flowers that make this plant remarkable so much as the very large heart-shaped leaves. They look soft and they really do feel like velvet. For this reason the plant is called Velvet Leaf (*Abutilon theophrasti*).

The large brown seed containers form a very attractive pattern. At one time these seed vessels were used to stamp decorations on butter and on pie crusts. For this reason the plant also became known as Butter-print and Pie-marker.

78

Queen Anne's Lace or Bird's Nest or Wild Carrot

At one time it was quite stylish for fashionable English ladies to use the lacy green leaves of Queen Anne's Lace (*Daucus carota*) for personal decoration, especially in their hair. This may be the origin of the name Queen Anne's Lace. However, some people claim that the name refers to the flowers, which resemble beautiful, delicate circles of lace. The white clusters are made up of many separate little· flowers arranged like a flat-topped umbrella. The one in the center is usually deep red or purple. According to legend, it represents a drop of blood shed by Queen Anne when she pricked her finger while making lace.

In late summer, when blossoming is over and the fruits begin to ripen, the sides of the flower head curl inward, creating a deep cup that resembles the nest of a bird. Thus, another common name is Bird's Nest.

This plant is closely related to our cultivated carrot, and its root is said to have many medicinal uses. Pull up a root and smell it. The sweet, carroty aroma is immediately recognizable and explains the plant's other common name, Wild Carrot.

Common Sunflower

According to Greek mythology, there was a water nymph named Clytië who decided one day to leave the ocean and visit the land. Clytië climbed to the top of Mount Olympus. There she saw the sun god Apollo and fell madly in love with him. But he loved someone else, and this made her very sad. Day after day, she did nothing but gaze at the sun from dawn to dusk—until she sank into the earth, developed roots, and changed into a flower. As the plant grew and blossomed, it always turned its face toward the sun, reflecting the rays of Clytië's beloved, Apollo. Because of this, the plant was named Sunflower (*Helianthus annuus*). The genus name comes from two Greek words, *helios* ("sun") and *anthos* ("flower"). The Sunflower is found throughout the United States and is the state flower of Kansas.

Wild Clematis or Traveler's Joy or Old Man's Beard

Wild Clematis (*Clematis virginiana*) grows along roads and woodland borders where it climbs about decorating trees, shrubs, fences, and old stone walls. The name Clematis comes from the Greek word *klema*, which means vine branch. Where the vine forms a heavy drapery over trees and shrubs, it provides a traveler with shelter from sun or rain. It also offers him the beauty of its fragrant clusters of white blossoms against dark green leaves, and thus it is called Traveler's Joy. The blossoms are later replaced by handsome feathery balls of seeds. Their white woolly appearance suggested a third common name, Old Man's Beard.

Index

Library of Congress Cataloging in Publication Data
Busch, Phyllis S.   Wildflowers and the stories behind their
names.   Includes index.
SUMMARY: Describes more than sixty familiar American
wildflowers and presents the stories behind their popular
names.
1. Wild flowers—United States—Juvenile literature. 2. Plant
names, Popular—Juvenile literature. [1. Wild flowers. 2. Plant
names, Popular]   I. Dowden, Anne Ophelia Todd, 1907-
II. Title.   QK115.B87   528'.13'0973   73-1351
ISBN 0-684-14820-X